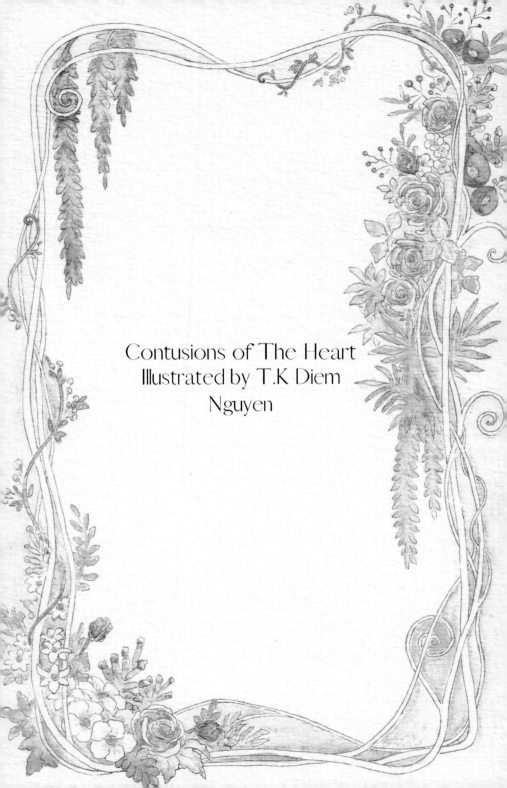

Contusions of The Heart
Illustrated by T.K Diem
Nguyen

TABLE OF CONTENTS

This book is dedicated to you.

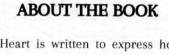

ABOUT THE BOOK

Contusions of the Heart is written to express how quickly emotions change with the damaging ways of the world. The contusions of heartbreak, loss, and rejection inflicted on a person, provoke uncertainty and turmoil. Happiness comes and goes, and my poetry brings to life the imperfections of a human being. Why do we love so hard? Why do we hate even harder? With a patient heart, your eyes will set light to visualize the words of pain along with the cuts and bruises and what life can feel like after they are healed. Our darkest moments should never be hidden. As I grow older, I may never understand the cause of empty feelings, even when I am at my best. Learning to understand that I can fill myself with love and hope, and surround myself with it as well, lets me know I oversee my growth. The sun does not ask the moon to shine when the night is over because he knows his purpose. You ought to reveal what hurts the most and accept it. Feel your way through adversity, passion, regret, and failure so you can start the journey of self-love. Free the mind by healing the contusions of your heart. I give you pain, love, and strength in words.

I can taste the peace in this sad place,
It sapor's my grandmother's cornbread.
It sounds like summer rain.
To be still in a controlled world full of dead walkers,
I celebrate not living on the end of some ones string.
My vision is blurred and cannot see those who
Intend to break my spirit.
I have outgrown a man that holds me in a closed fist,
My growth will not be stunted.
A woman with an ill mouth against my well-being
Will provoke deafness to my ears.
The touch of a stranger is forbidden.
My energy is not accessible to
Those who have not earned it.

Accepting Peace

The country is where my heart resides, where my body is still,
And my mind is aligned.
I could not cope with the hustle of the city,
So, I cried many nights in a studio apartment
That I kept empty.
Harmful energy persuaded my thoughts after the devil
Greeted me with vices.
He spent time with me just to collect my tears,
And laugh at my fears,
Until I met a man who introduced me to the sun.
His presence shined on me and identified the
Imbalance of my breath.
He taught me how to breathe so I can succeed,
Showing me that I belong anywhere the earth moves.
I felt myself let go;
On this day I gave him my sorrow.
He carried it with poise, never letting it dictate his strength.
I have accepted love and my heart did not have to bargain
With intellectual power.
The seeds planted inside of me will nourish my womb,
Morning, noon, and night.
The root of my foundation he has become,
An absorbing and transporting love without condition.
He is now where my heart resides,
Where my body is still, and my mind is aligned.

We Met in the City

When you were immured by your demons,
I loved you still,
Followed long and dishonest paths to reserve
Placement in your life.
Your wounds I fed with my weakness.
I felt the deadly bite of you wolfing
My heart into a great divide.
A crippled mountain is where I stand alone,
Touching wind that never blows.
Somehow, I am chilled into stillness,
And confronted by the deep stories you
Disposed to my soft mind.
Your unforgettable spirit has me
Entwined by your seasoned memories.
My cries belong to you;
I am enraged by the confinement of our defiled history.
My life has imploded into oblivion,
Becoming nothingness as you continue to have a
Purpose in your breath.
And still, I love you.

Coddled Heart

9

The dreams you once had are unattainable,
Followed by the rived jealousy blocking your potential to inspire.
Their words are gospel, concealing your efforts.
The whip around your neck shows them you are unworthy of growth.
How did you end up so sad, devoted to someone else's vision?
Dismissing goals held dear, losing yourself is what you fear.
The mirrors in every room are supposed to reflect the light
Inside of you,
But they are covered with wallpaper.
Too many years of letting insecurities guide the
Path to your destruction.
You have become afraid your chin will expose true sadness.
Your greatest accomplishment is running away from your happiness.
It is never too late to recognize your value and magnify the
Butterfly inside of the woman who hides inside her cocoon.

Hapless Woman

The pages were as blank as the stare you donated before saying goodbye.
You had nothing left to give after dedicating yourself to me.
Your heart was tempered with,
Lessening its gift to love completely,
Starved by your touch, and ashamed of the words lost
Because of your absence.
Wherever you roamed, my tender lyrics followed.
I revisit our past moments when the days long for the night,
Yearning for your presence like the bird's passion in the spring.
My diary keeps the secrets of the love I have held for you all these years.
It mocks a bottomless well, promising to never run out.

A Letter of Grievance

Shine down on my pretty brown.
Vulnerable in the night,
I rely on you to glisten on my darkness.
Shape the ugly me you see into a shadowed beauty.
So high and radiant, it is impossible to weep with loneliness.
Being underneath you creates a feeling of ecstasy.
In your presence,
I stand still, heartening the glow forced upon me.
Crescent moon,
Your brilliance overrides the melanism of the small hour with direction.
Your lucid design has aided me with trust.
Receiving insight that my continued living is not in vain.
I am indebted to your afterglow,
In awe of your commitment to guide me with your softness.

Clever Moon

I knew a boy whose love reached a depth of meaning
Science could never define.
My heart had endured a maelstrom effect because of his love.
Stumbling over words before his kiss graced my lips,
His affection had me unsteady.
A young man who sought love when he simply held
My hand under his apple tree.
He did not create his way of loving based on the pain
Felt from the line of families that discarded him as if
He was replaceable.
Before they took away his words, I will never forget
The ones that are stuck in the past:
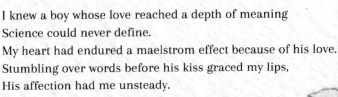
"No one teaches you that there are memories a tree preserves.
They return the favor and give me life;
I learn from nature, not humans and that is why I
Will always love you."
He saw matters of the heart for what it was,
Unconditional and genuine,
Giving a hopelessly romantic love as soft as silk.

A Man's Virtue

In my dreams, he glorified my existence, aspiring to
Marry me and my broken steps.
He promised to rebuild, to be grounded,
Without the need to fight for a way up.
The countless times he visited mind's eye.
"Are you calling out for me?"
I would spend many days daydreaming about him
Becoming my reality.
I lost sight of the real world, and was conned into
Searching for the perfect man;
A lonely woman who craves intimacy,
Devoted to a man that was
Created out of conscious need.

Rose-Colored Glasses

16

Speak freely so I can meditate on the rhythm of your words.
Be my sweet fruit harvesting to my liking.
Take time to understand the affinity
Of the deep-rooted issues to show your care.
All this time, I have been hesitant to share.
The floorboards meet my knees,
As I beg you not to be frightened by the
Imperfections that have caused me to deflect.
Speak fluently with love.
Imitate my lavender and calm me with your presence.
Come closer.
And be my fragrance.

Love Language

Our bodies gracefully touch sensing ones
Eagerness to be wanted.
You are adorned by the flowering
Of my hidden waters.
I have surrendered my body,
Patiently Blossoming inside of your garden.
Kisses of inspiration, yet a reminder your lips
Have the after taste of pain.
With your collected work of heavy hearts,
The pieces that left you broken I will
Familiarize myself with.
The love that you pour inside me is novelty,
I feel you flowing through me poetically.

The Beginning of Us

He emphasized my flaws and discontinued loving my all.
I sensed feelings of rejection by someone I invited into my
Element of comfort during his downfall.
My guard was down within an instant.
Intuition advised me to keep building for protection until
He earned his pension.
Virtue begged me to believe in him; I listened.
With a lack of contributions, accomplishments did not exist.
I gave life to his pride and forced intimacy.
Fantasy tailing, idolizing the image of what could be.
The hand dealt has been withdrawn,
Resenting being in a relationship that was never meant to be.

Broken Compass

Days grow slow and I sit alone on an old swing they
Used to beg to play on, with undying excitement.
My unsettled thoughts are pumped with the idea of
My boys being young again.
Restless days affected my quality of life, and I
Harbored grudges for simply being needed,
Secretly haunted by those nights when their clingy
Nature was unserved.
The boughs would hit the windowpane in sympathy
With the roaring storm,
Frightened, with their hearts in their mouth.
I gave in to mankind's victimizing game and chose
Apathy, blaming them for having to need me.
Nurturing a child was not a gift of mine.
Pretending to be a mother, I was a counterfeit.
I took pills just to be patient, supportive, and humble.
Consistency was not something I mastered;
I could be a chameleon when my mood changed.
If those days were granted back to me,
I would move heaven and earth to furnish their
Hearts with bravery.

Paper Tigers

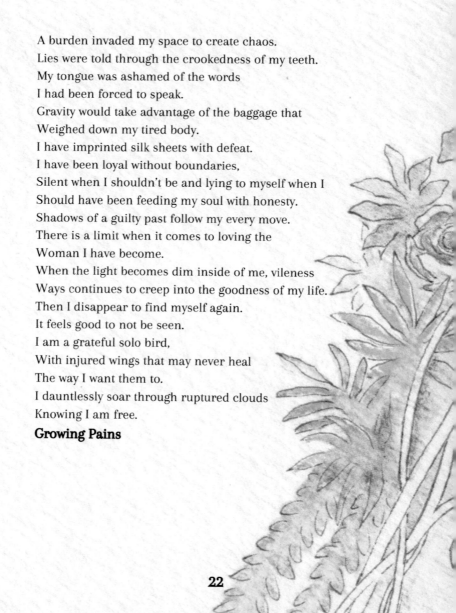

A burden invaded my space to create chaos.
Lies were told through the crookedness of my teeth.
My tongue was ashamed of the words
I had been forced to speak.
Gravity would take advantage of the baggage that
Weighed down my tired body.
I have imprinted silk sheets with defeat.
I have been loyal without boundaries,
Silent when I shouldn't be and lying to myself when I
Should have been feeding my soul with honesty.
Shadows of a guilty past follow my every move.
There is a limit when it comes to loving the
Woman I have become.
When the light becomes dim inside of me, vileness
Ways continues to creep into the goodness of my life.
Then I disappear to find myself again.
It feels good to not be seen.
I am a grateful solo bird,
With injured wings that may never heal
The way I want them to.
I dauntlessly soar through ruptured clouds
Knowing I am free.

Growing Pains

Nights of somberness have always crept on you,
Leaving you desolate.
Yet, you persist in sheltering my
Faith so that it never wavers.
I have watched you cast away a society of vultures
Preying on your weakness.

When I begin to lose my supply of hope,
You become my hade of solace amid exhaustion,
Sun-flowering my life that you protect with the
Nourishment of unconditional love.

My Island, My Centerpiece

24

A gentle woman with admirable attributes.
Her merciful but steady hands are raised to the free sky as
The breeze brushes her fine braids.
The clouds slowly collide with one another,
Accepting a soft abundance.
When the sun rises, it praises her ebony.
Heaven's star began to have an emollient effect on her skin,
Hiding flaws that bear trauma only she can see.
With no more secrets to store, she journeys through a portal,
Exposing her true divinity.
A brave-hearted woman with indestructible steps, you will see
Her amble through life with
Elegance, but she demands to be recognized by the
Strength reigned upon.
A poetic woman once stuck in a rough draft for years,
Rewriting and editing the essence of who she is.
Nourishing her worth with positivity, knowing it is not easy,
Through the process of healing.
She is a God-fearing woman who is finalizing
Her story from within.
Her testimony does not end as she bows her head in
Repentance of her sins.

Living Poetry

Let me know that you are okay.
I know you're going through a lot.
I can try not to care but I do.
She was just for a moment,
You are for a lifetime.
You matter to me.
Don't shut me out.
I have more invested in you than anyone else.
And when I feel you're not alright,
I am affected.
Text me back so I know you have read my message.

Fake Remorse

In a moment, I was in love, only once did I dedicate my touch.
It was easy to lose you in the empty space
Where you once occupied.
For a month of Sundays,
I have avoided isolation because it feels like a death grip.
Angry at the sun, I run into the solitude of
The garden I am growing in.
My dying stems contain the shadows of
A black cloud that robs him of any shine.
I believe the longer he accepts my estranged energy,
The easier it will be to give in to my cries and to adhere to
My disavowed lies.

Self-Serving Love

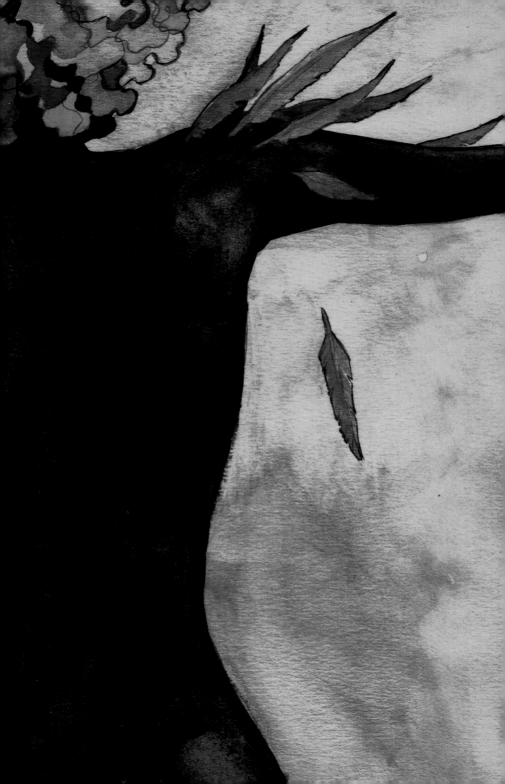

The affections of your heart were not infinite,
Detained by your tall talk,
And worshiping every word.
The engraved marks revealed on my arm reminded
Me of the unschooled girl who thought your
Love was her boundless sea.
A man's fool,
And afraid to fly,
As I trusted words of distortion,
Rituals are sung to let go until the
Attachments of you become unraveled and
Coveted no more.
"I am not your scarlet macaw,
I will no longer be held captive by
The feeding of your lies."

Free from Deceit

I left and returned, only humbled to have left his doorstep.
He found ways to keep me mellow, surrogating your presence.
I felt like his double rainbow after our skies completed its cry.
My comfort was the light he saw when all
I could see was gloom.
His desire was for me to relinquish my oath to the vows that
Were once the law to my heart.
Time continues and trust fades.
Change is promised.
My waist you grip so tight, all while wailing on your knees to
Accept its potential.
Why blacken my inner peace with your impassible mentality?
I denied the broken promises,
And finally refusing to be conjured by the cunning intentions
Of a man I have always loved more than myself.

Behind Hand

The creation of you has my body in beautiful agony.
Unrested guilt has swallowed me into the throat of depression,
And I digest it as sorrow.
I stand in front of roses;
I hope it will instill an essence of calmness
From my heart to yours.
A dark red rose stands out as I see her losing petals,
Pleading with nature to help her thrive again.
A sudden feeling of inspiration grazes my frown and
I give it a half smile.
There is a gentle touch at the center of my stomach
My hands wandered without notice.
And I whisper *"I will always be your rainwater."*
Forever and a lifetime, your unrevealed soul will be
Showered with care from a mother
That lives for tomorrow.
Because you exist.

The Genesis of You

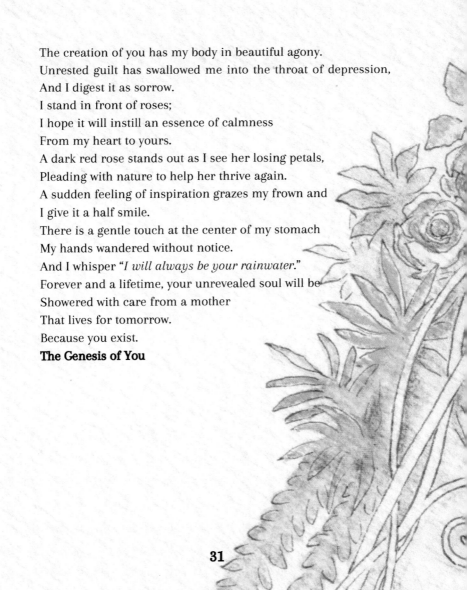

You drove down dark back roads,
Musing the lyrics to your favorite song.
You always liked to take a long way home.
I kissed the side of your lips and held mine there until you
Parked your car near your hoarded but charming backyard.
You told me the story of how your father lost your mother.
All he had left was his son and the things she left behind.
We held hands up the grassy hill, a sunless night surrounded
By broad fragranced evergreens.
You will never know what that peak of perfection meant to me.
The air felt our skin as we floated close inside of your
Hammock, butterfly high,
And gazing at the open sky.
Last Night's Beau

I am approached by his strong hands,
And his touch compels me to stray.
I lust after the thought of myself
Clinging to his bed sheets.
The shaking of my body caused by the penetration of his
Manhood has summoned me to be submissive.
I am commanded by his air;
The will to leave is non-existent.
My reluctance to deny his
Sexual gestures is seen but ignored.
At this moment, it is satisfying because
Tomorrow I will want more.

Shameful Kisses

You are deprived of my presence,
You have been denying me since your fickle adolescence.
I am known for teaching men lessons.
All those women you let steal your color, you look lifeless.
May I revive you from the last sister who left you breathless?
Survive for me, by making me your everything.
Give my love a taste.
Night resembles my bitter skin,
But when you take a bite to the core, my juices are sweet.
Put your seeds inside of me and take a
Journey into my underworld.
I'll nourish you as you nourish me with our watermelon love.

Fruitful Divine

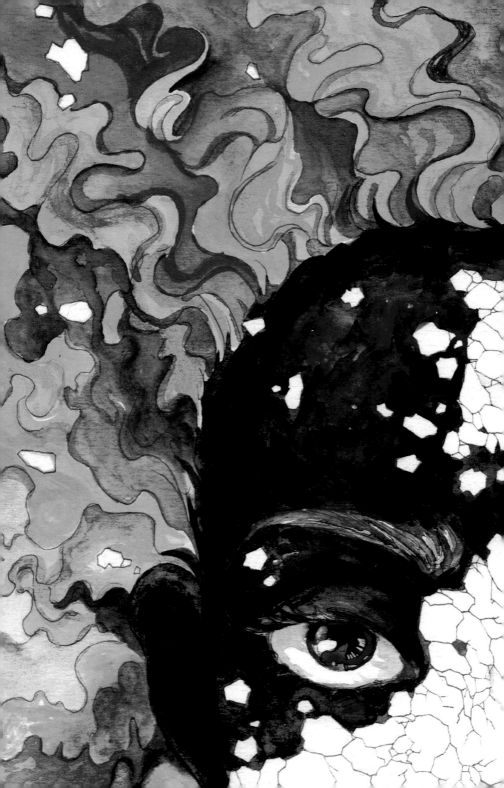